50 POP SONGS FOR KIDS

Available for
FLUTE, OBOE, CLARINET, ALTO SAX, TENOR SAX, TRUMPET, HORN,
TROMBONE, VIOLIN, VIOLA, CELLO, RECORDER, and MALLET PERCUSSION

ISBN 978-1-70510-736-2

HAL•LEONARD®

Visit Hal Leonard Online at
www.halleonard.com

T0057797

Contact us:
Hal Leonard
7777 West Bluemound Road
Milwaukee, WI 53213
Email: info@halleonard.com

In Europe, contact:
Hal Leonard Europe Limited
42 Wigmore Street
Marylebone, London, W1U 2RN
Email: info@halleonardeurope.com

In Australia, contact:
Hal Leonard Australia Pty. Ltd.
4 Lentara Court
Cheltenham, Victoria, 3192 Australia
Email: info@halleonard.com.au

ANOTHER ONE BITES THE DUST

ALTO SAX

Words and Music by
JOHN DEACON

BELIEVER

ALTO SAX

Words and Music by DAN REYNOLDS, WAYNE SERMON, BEN McKEE, DANIEL PLATZMAN, JUSTIN TRANTOR, MATTIAS LARSSON and ROBIN FREDRICKSSON

CALL ME MAYBE

ALTO SAX

Words and Music by CARLY RAE JEPSEN,
JOSHUA RAMSAY and TAVISH CROWE

5

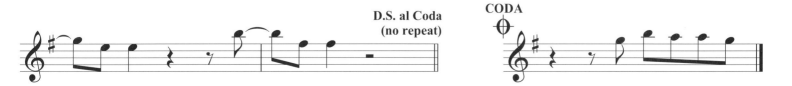

CAN'T STOP THE FEELING!
from TROLLS

ALTO SAX

Words and Music by JUSTIN TIMBERLAKE,
MAX MARTIN and SHELLBACK

EVERYTHING IS AWESOME
(Awesome Remixx!!!)
from THE LEGO MOVIE

ALTO SAX

Words by SHAWN PATTERSON
Music by ANDREW SAMBERG,
JORMA TACCONE, AKIVA SCHAFFER,
JOSHUA BARTHOLOMEW, LISA HARRITON
and SHAWN PATTERSON

DANCE MONKEY

ALTO SAX

Words and Music by
TONI WATSON

DON'T FEAR THE REAPER

ALTO SAX

Words and Music by
DONALD ROESER

DON'T STOP BELIEVIN'

ALTO SAX

Words and Music by STEVE PERRY,
NEAL SCHON and JONATHAN CAIN

Moderate Rock

FEEL IT STILL

ALTO SAX

Words and Music by JOHN GOURLEY,
ZACH CAROTHERS, JASON SECHRIST, ERIC HOWK,
KYLE O'QUIN, BRIAN HOLLAND, FREDDIE GORMAN,
GEORGIA DOBBINS, ROBERT BATEMAN, WILLIAM GARRETT,
JOHN HILL and ASA TACCONE

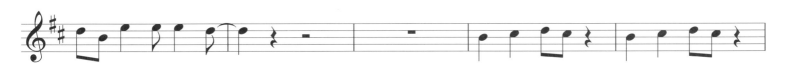

FIGHT SONG

ALTO SAX

Words and Music by RACHEL PLATTEN
and DAVE BASSETT

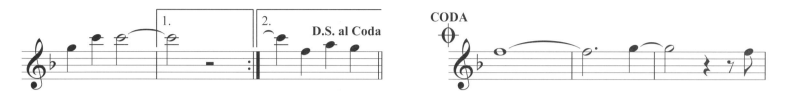

FOREVER YOUNG

ALTO SAX

Words and Music by ROD STEWART,
KEVIN SAVIGAR, JIM CREGAN
and BOB DYLAN

FREE FALLIN'

ALTO SAX

Words and Music by TOM PETTY
and JEFF LYNNE

HALLELUJAH

ALTO SAX

Words and Music by
LEONARD COHEN

HAPPY
from DESPICABLE ME 2

ALTO SAX

Words and Music by
PHARRELL WILLIAMS

HIGH HOPES

ALTO SAX

Words and Music by BRENDON URIE,
SAMUEL HOLLANDER, WILLIAM LOBBAN BEAN,
JONAS JEBERG, JACOB SINCLAIR,
JENNY OWEN YOUNGS, ILSEY JUBER,
LAUREN PRITCHARD and TAYLA PARX

Moderately

To Coda

D.S. al Coda

CODA

HOUND DOG

ALTO SAX

Words and Music by JERRY LEIBER
and MIKE STOLLER

LOUIE, LOUIE

ALTO SAX

Words and Music by
RICHARD BERRY

I DON'T CARE

ALTO SAX

Words and Music by ED SHEERAN,
JUSTIN BIEBER, FRED GIBSON,
JASON BOYD, MAX MARTIN
and SHELLBACK

Syncopated Pop

IN THE AIR TONIGHT

ALTO SAX

Words and Music by
PHIL COLLINS

INTO THE GROOVE

ALTO SAX

Words and Music by STEPHEN BRAY
and MADONNA CICCONE

INTO THE UNKNOWN
from FROZEN 2

ALTO SAX

Music and Lyrics by KRISTEN ANDERSON-LOPEZ
and ROBERT LOPEZ

Mysteriously, in 2

LET IT BE

ALTO SAX

Words and Music by JOHN LENNON
PAUL McCARTNEY

LET'S GET IT STARTED

ALTO SAX

Words and Music by WILL ADAMS,
ALLAN PINEDA, JAIME GOMEZ,
MICHAEL FRATANTUNO, GEORGE PAJON JR.
and TERENCE YOSHIAKI GRAVES

To Coda

D.S. al Coda

CODA

THE MIDDLE

ALTO SAX

Words and Music by SARAH AARONS,
MARCUS LOMAX, JORDAN JOHNSON,
ANTON ZASLAVSKI, KYLE TREWARTHA,
MICHAEL TREWARTHA and STEFAN JOHNSON

A MILLION DREAMS
from THE GREATEST SHOWMAN

ALTO SAX

Words and Music by BENJ PASEK
and JUSTIN PAUL

NO TEARS LEFT TO CRY

ALTO SAX

Words and Music by ARIANA GRANDE,
SAVAN KOTECHA, MAX MARTIN
and ILYA

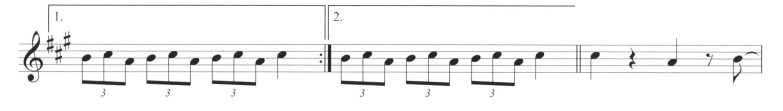

(small notes optional)

OCEAN EYES

ALTO SAX

Words and Music by
FINNEAS O'CONNELL

PERFECT

ALTO SAX

Words and Music by
ED SHEERAN

OLD TOWN ROAD
(Remix)

ALTO SAX

Words and Music by TRENT REZNOR,
BILLY RAY CYRUS, JOCELYN DONALD,
ATTICUS ROSS, KIOWA ROUKEMA
and MONTERO LAMAR HILL

PARTY IN THE U.S.A.

ALTO SAX

Words and Music by JESSICA CORNISH,
LUKASZ GOTTWALD and CLAUDE KELLY

Moderate Pop

PROUD MARY

ALTO SAX

Words and Music by
JOHN FOGERTY

RESPECT

ALTO SAX

Words and Music by
OTIS REDDING

REWRITE THE STARS

from THE GREATEST SHOWMAN

ALTO SAX

Words and Music by BENJ PASEK
and JUSTIN PAUL

SPIRIT
from THE LION KING 2019

ALTO SAX

Written by TIMOTHY McKENZIE,
ILYA SALMANZADEH and BEYONCÉ

SCARS TO YOUR BEAUTIFUL

ALTO SAX

Words and Music by ALESSIA CARACCIOLO,
WARREN FELDER, COLERIDGE TILLMAN
and ANDREW WANSEL

Moderate Pop beat

SUCKER

ALTO SAX

Words and Music by NICK JONAS,
JOSEPH JONAS, MILES ALE,
MUSTAFA AHMED, RYAN TEDDER,
LOUIS BELL, ADAM FEENEY,
KEVIN JONAS and HOMER STEINWEISS

SURFIN' U.S.A.

ALTO SAX

Words and Music by
CHUCK BERRY

Solid Shuffle beat

SWEET HOME ALABAMA

ALTO SAX

Words and Music by RONNIE VAN ZANT,
ED KING and GARY ROSSINGTON

TOMORROW
from the Musical Production ANNIE

ALTO SAX

Lyric by MARTIN CHARNIN
Music by CHARLES STROUSE

Moderately slow

A THOUSAND MILES

ALTO SAX

Words and Music by
VANESSA CARLTON

TWIST AND SHOUT

ALTO SAX

Words and Music by BERT RUSSELL
and PHIL MEDLEY

WE WILL ROCK YOU

ALTO SAX

Words and Music by
BRIAN MAY

VIVA LA VIDA

ALTO SAX

Words and Music by GUY BERRYMAN,
JON BUCKLAND, WILL CHAMPION
and CHRIS MARTIN

Moderately

WE ARE NEVER EVER
GETTING BACK TOGETHER

ALTO SAX

Words and Music by TAYLOR SWIFT,
MAX MARTIN and SHELLBACK

To Coda

D.S. al Coda

CODA

WHAT ABOUT US

ALTO SAX

Words and Music by ALECIA MOORE,
STEVE MAC and JOHNNY McDAID

WISH YOU WERE HERE

ALTO SAX

Words and Music by ROGER WATERS
and DAVID GILMOUR

WHATEVER IT TAKES

ALTO SAX

Words and Music by DAN REYNOLDS,
WAYNE SERMON, BEN McKEE,
DANIEL PLATZMAN and JOEL LITTLE

Moderately

Y.M.C.A.

ALTO SAX

Words and Music by JACQUES MORALI,
HENRI BELOLO and VICTOR WILLIS

YOU CAN CALL ME AL

ALTO SAX

Words and Music by
PAUL SIMON

YOU WILL BE FOUND

from DEAR EVAN HANSEN

ALTO SAX

Music and Lyrics by BENJ PASEK
and JUSTIN PAUL

Moderately slow